SHELBY MARIE

To *W*

Moonbeams

TO WALK ON MOONBEAMS

SHELBY MARIE

To Walk on Moonbeams

Written by Shelby Marie

This is for anyone,
for everyone,
for all who may stumble,
for all who may need it.

CONTENTS

DARK

s a l t   w a t e r

He says he loves me.
These words I drink in too big mouthfuls.

I'm doing the same thing I always do
and I loathe myself for it
because no matter how desperately
I want to stop falling,
I am already in motion.

This love is everything I've ever wanted
and at times it is still too much.

I am afraid of loss,
of holding happiness in my hands
and then living in the absence
of everything I've ever wanted.

Don't let go.

Don't.

Do you think we could make it
if we dance carefully in the flames,
if we burn up at only our edges
and then lick each other's wounds between battles?

Do you think we could exist
with this fire consuming our insides,
charring our hearts
and making closeness unbearable?

Do you think,
if we love hard enough,
if we're cautious enough,
if we hold on to this balance,
do you think we'll make it?

In all of our confusion
there's still one thing I know.
I am willing to try.

If I give him room to grow,
will he give me space to breathe?

Do you think we could exist
close enough to love,
far enough for comfort?

I'd give him all of my oxygen
if he felt it a struggle to breathe.

Hush now. It'll be all right.
Never mind what'll become of me.

Don't you dare give up on me.
We haven't pointed out
all of the constellations in the sky.
We haven't danced in morning's dewy grass
like you promised.
We have not yet kissed
in a valley of fragrant flowers
with the moon above us,
but a crescent in the nighttime.
Don't you slip away with your darkness.

Take my hand and hold on tightly.
I am ready to run,
no matter how long or far,
even if the stones get stuck in our shoes
and we bleed through the soles.
Even if we're screaming before the stillness,
I will not let you go.
I refuse to let you be consumed
by your monsters.

My heart is a sword and I will fight for you.
I will love you through this storm
and the next,
and the next.

I love you.
I will save you.
Just promise you won't let go.

I am not afraid of him leaving.

I am afraid of the things
I might do once he's gone.

I heard him say her name
when it was I who took his breath away.

Perhaps it is true that some loves never die.

Speak to me as autumn does its leaves,
passionately, as our time might be fleeting.

Do not speak to me in heavy summer tongues,
as though we might remain in the humid, sticky air
for our entire lives long.

I do not need to bloom again,
and I am not frosty cold.
I have thawed and calmed my rapid heart
so give me changing colours and crisp air.

Remind me that we might not have forever,
but that where we are right now
is exactly where we're meant to be.

There is hope for us yet.
I refuse to believe that this is the end.

Imagine the world a little differently.

You wrap your slender fingers
around a coffee cup to cool them down.

The birds sing softly before you fall asleep.
When you wake, the moon is rising too.

It all feels a little off balance.

This is a world without you.

So stay.
Help me to keep my footing on this downhill slope.
I'm afraid of the darkness at the end of falling
and your heart makes mine feel brave.

Without you I am a wildfire, consuming.
Without, I am a starless sky, a day without sunshine,
the darkness, the cold, lonely, broken.

If my love for him is not enough
then no part of me is,
because I have never loved anything
as fiercely as I've loved him.

- Not even myself

I wanted to be more.
He said I was enough.

The snow sparkles
where the streetlight's illumination
was brave enough to reach out and touch it,
brave enough to embrace
the pinprick points of ice
that would bite at skin if they were able,
if they could.

If I could,
I'd watch a million sunsets with him,
but as it is, we've only this one.

So kiss these lifelong frozen lips
like you mean it.

Hold me.
Hold me until the coral colours
disappear over the horizon.
Hold me into the nighttime,
until the temperature sinks
and the day fades away.

Kiss me like the cold won't bite.
Kiss me like we'll always have tomorrow,
even if we don't,
even if we should.

The snow sparkles beautifully,
but it's cold.
He calls me beautiful and I know,
I know I am just like those pinpricks of ice,
beauty that bites at the touch.

I'm cold, come back.
It doesn't have to be like this.
Even winter thaws into spring.
Soon summer will come
and things will be better, warmer.
Fall is breathtaking.
You and I together are the same.
Our frostbitten fear
of this arctic cold season,
it won't last.
We'll get past this.
Come back.

Loving him won't make him stay.
Loving him won't stop me from losing him.

It didn't.

LONELY

I waited for him to come back,
but love is not like the change of a season,
the moving of night into day.
It is never guaranteed.

Our love, it was never carved in stone.

He, like fresh cut flowers, was sorcery,
beautiful until inevitably rotten.

We are too much candy on movie dates,
nightmares from the sugar rush,
and holding each other close
when the bad dreams wake us.

Just because it makes you feel alive,
it doesn't mean it's good for you.

He wove a spiderweb of doubt
with gossamer threads,
tentative, tedious lines
of a story with too many words
when the only one left to say now was
s o r r y.

I drink until the room spins
and stop only when I forget
the reasons I wanted
to find myself this lost.

I drink until his ghost is gone,
and I can't remember
how to form the syllables
that make up the likes of his name.

I drink until I've escaped his chains,
and I've forgotten all of the ways
in which I still love him.

Will I always love him?

If you're going to
watch me unravel,
at least untie the knots.

I'm still learning
how to breathe softly
instead of in gulps.

I'm still holding out
for the kind of love
you want to decorate your walls,
the kind you keep
in perfect polaroid frames.

I'm still learning
that not every breath will be easy,
but the next ones, they'll come.
They'll come and I'll have learned
not to gasp when I see him.

They'll come and the lesson
will have been worth it.

Don't let the butterflies in your stomach upset it.
Don't let him sweep you up in his storm
because when he kisses you, it'll feel like magic.

It's only ever too late when you realize
that aftertaste is poison.

Always remember
that the air you're breathing,
it's a blessing,
that your next breath
might not come so easily.

I remind myself every day
that he's not coming back.

I must remember to breathe.

Tell me, if you could see into my future,
what do you think I might become?

Do you think I could be happy?

I just feel a little out of place,
like I'm walking along
the bottom of the ocean
with an oxygen tank
that's about to run out.

It's like I'm on a plane that's crashing
and I'm the only one without a parachute.

I feel like I'm standing
in the middle of a crosswalk,
the hand is glaring red
and tells me to stop
so I freeze in place,
but I swear only moments before
the world was in a hurried frenzy,
walking about.

I'm not sure if I should call out to you
and hope that my muted bubbles of air
cause enough of a stir when they reach the surface
or if asking you to return will only kill me quicker.

I tried to choose the right words,
opened my mouth to feel it full of cobwebs,
empty except for the dusting of our history.

But I opened my mouth to say what?
To beg him to stay?
To apologize again?
To yell and scream in frustration?

I closed it, bit my lip and watched him walk away.
Maybe there wasn't anything left to say now.

Goodbye,
before paper cuts become broken bones,
before broken bones become lost limbs,
before I lose even more of myself
in chaos that crept in slowly.

LEAVING

They say the glass is half full.

I say half empty
because I know what it's like
to feel that something is missing.

It fucking hurts.
This emptiness.

The day he left,
I saw the thunder.

His eyes are grey storm clouds.
I search for them in the downpour.

SHELBY MARIE

My heart is bitter
like the bite on the breeze,
his is colder
than the coming winter.

I can't sleep.
These thoughts of him are restless.

We are ravens
as dark as night
in mourning.

The morning
will take the grief away.

I keep telling myself
the night always ends.

Everything ends.
Sadness is temporary.

I miss myself before the heartbreak.

I still feel the ghost of him
trailing phantom kisses
across my collarbone,
gently up my neck,
leaving ice on my lips
that takes my breath away.

I still hear him whisper
"*I love you,*" before I fall asleep.

Loving too little leaves you lonely.
Loving too much brings you pain.

I've yet to find a balance.

You fix this with tenderness.
You fix this with forgiveness,
with love.

But I think that is
an entirely different language
than one we'll both understand.

I found love in the lost.
I found home in the dark.

But I think I'm ready for this night to end.

I have tried countless ways
to make myself feel something.

I have sliced open skin
to feel the sting of endorphins,
starved to feel the acid
churn in my stomach,
loved so I might know how it feels
to have a heart shattered
instead of simply frozen.

And all of these wounds
have still left me numb.

M.E.N.D.I.N.G

If you're not sewing yourself back together,
you're pulling the threads apart.

I want to walk on moonbeams
and sip soft sunlight.

I want to be free,
but I've only ever felt alive
while I was tied down to earth by him.

Fall in love if you have to
or save yourself if you're able.

I am up late night,
midnight rolls around.
The stars rise,
greet the moon
like time was never lost
between them,
like some loves
never die
even though they do.

I will beg the ghost of him
to reach into my chest
and slow my beating heart's rhythm
to a gentler song,
because I can't stand the pain
that shoots through me
when it remembers that he's gone.

I am a beautiful mess
of skin and bones,
pretty porcelain
on the verge of breaking.

The moon howls too.
I hear her in my sleep.
She is lonely.

I guess between
her,
myself,
and this tired
h e a r t
that makes three.

And good things come in threes.
But the sound of her breaking
makes me worried about
how much longer
all of us will have to wait
for something better.

If I could ask just one last thing,
it'd be that I could let him go
as autumn does its leaves.

I hope he finds someone
who makes him feel
like even the saddest parts of life
are worth living.

Even though he'll never deserve them.

He'll miss me.
Even in uncertainty, this I know.

I really did love him,
but I was younger then.

Sometimes we don't deserve to be forgiven.
And sometimes we are anyways.

I'm ready to let him go.

The fire crackles
as it begins to grow,
spits out embers
like it's choking too.
Maybe it is.

The flames lick higher.
They char all that they can reach,
wrap around trunks of trees, strangling.

The heat boils my blood
and the thumping in my head
is almost too much.
It is all too much.

This wildfire is spreading
and I say,
let it
B U R N.

HEALING

Death spoke low as I bowed deeply before it,
as though its voice, its words, its ideas,
were a dream, a silhouette, untouchable.

As though it were an epiphany
of mortality's nature
to dance delicately, in and out of reach,
Death spoke deliberately and I shivered.

"Come."

"No. I'm not ready to go."

Everything I do is a choice.
My choice.
And loving him is up to me.

I will not love what isn't good for me.

He left
and there is this cavity
like a chasm in my chest.

I scream in agony,
startled awake from nightmares
that grow in his absence.

But this is only temporary
because self-love heals.
Self-love will fix this.

I've been called beautiful
while I was falling apart,
as if the word could somehow
stitch me back together.

It is not the same
as a needle and thread.
The word *beautiful*
is not made up of tender hands
that work over wounds
with tenacious love.

Beautiful does not fix you.

Calling me beautiful
while I'm at my worst
tells me that he likes me better
when I'm broken,
when he has a pretty little play thing
to tinker with.

This is best,
when I am strong and brave.
This is beautiful,
this version of me that doesn't need him
to trail behind my heels,
picking up the pieces
I leave scattered wherever I go.

I don't need him
to make me feel beautiful anymore.

There is comfort in the dark and quiet.
I might stay awhile.
I might watch the stars and moon.
I might close my eyes for a short rest.

The sun is blindingly bright.
It burns my skin and leaves it angry red.
I need to let that fire go.

I need something that'll be good for me.

He's not going to always be there for me.

But I don't need him to save myself.

Maybe,
just maybe,
a fresh start is exactly what I need.

Maybe he isn't meant to be a part of it.

I do not have to shiver in the cold.
I can look to the light.
I can face this.

There is a fire in my eyes.
It burns bright in the nighttime.
It is relentless.
I am the same.

Fear is only as strong as it is allowed to be.
I am stronger than this.

I do not need to fear my monsters.
I do not need to be afraid.

Morning will come.
I will survive this.

Believing I am worth the battle
is how I'll win the war.

The shouts will become echoes.
They will fade and I will be okay.

Although the world might be unforgiving,
I might have to scale mountains with jagged edges,
I might have to swim across oceans
that stretch on past islands
with darkness nesting at their shores,
I might have to wander in his absence,
still I'll carry on.

I'll see lights in full colour.
I'll move with a backbone straightened and strong
until I find a place that feels like home.
A place where I can rest
without nightmares threatening.

I'll search until I've found a place
where rampikes are given rain
so they might try to start again.

The clouds will part.
The storm will end.
Even thunder can't rumble indefinitely.

I am not my shadow.
I am more than my darkness.

While my wounds won't heal entirely,
this I know,

all
scars
fade.

Forgive me,
I cannot yet remember
how I used to love myself,
but I am trying.

If I tell you all of my secrets,
could you do something small for me?

Take them away and hide them.
Lock them in a cage and destroy the key.
Throw these thoughts into waves
that are racing away from the shore.

Set me free.
Set me free.
Give me wings.

There is more to me than flesh and bones.
I am heart and soul,
memories and hard fought wars.

I am wonderstruck and wild.
I am freedom and victory.

And I am brave enough to try again.

I was dreaming in pastel colours,
pretending the world was softer,
less jagged than I feared it might be.
But I've woken,
and slumber did not do justice
to the world my eyes are now seeing anew.

The world is vibrant.
It is fiery red when love strikes.
It is the saddest, deepest blue
after goodbyes break us.

There are sunshine rays of hope
that break through the cloud cover
when hearts remember
that the bearable kinds of goodbyes
are only ever temporary.

I am in awe of the magenta sky at dawn,
of the branches that sway
with the crisp morning breeze.
The day is green with envy,
the trees are jealous of the footing I've found,
of this freedom I do not dare let go of.

The world is changing.
It is not soft petals and forgiving, dewy grass.
It is slipping and still finding reason to stand after.
It is pulling thorns from your side and still trying again.

It is dancing in the flames, fighting to stay,
even if the colours are too bright,
even if the day is not as softly shaded
as those sickly sweet dreams I'd clung to.

The world is changing and I,
I am waking. *I am getting better.*

If you look on the bright side,
sunlight starts to shine through.

Climb until the fall will break you.
Climb further still.
The view is beautiful up here.

This is me weathering the storm.
This is me being brave.
This is me at war.

I like to call this self-love.

I held the moon in my hands,
cradled it like an infant in need of tender love.

But the stars felt out of place and
the night was so dark that I sent her back home.

We cannot hold forever to any one thing.
Letting go only means we've been lucky enough
to have held on at all.

I know that the good things aren't going to last.
Nothing ever really lasts.
But that doesn't mean I should give up.
It doesn't mean I should stand in the shade
when there are streamers of sunlight
trying to reach me.
Just because I cannot have this forever,
it doesn't mean I shouldn't hold on for now.

What I'm trying to tell you,
what I'm trying to remind myself,

l i v e.

So maybe it's not beautiful,
maybe it's not perfect,
not a display of fireworks,
brilliant paintings hung on walls,
matching socks strung on the line,
that blow in the breeze,
things that work so easily
without even trying.

But right now is not forever
and time tends to mend all that is broken.

Maybe it's not perfect now,
but someday,
someday it'll be grand.

HESITANT

I suppose giving up means
I'm not willing to try again.

But I think things could be different this time.
I'm not the same as I was before.

And you are not him.

A love story

"I'm lonely," he said.

"It's okay," she told him.
"I have a little bit of love left to give."

We found each other because we needed to.

And now I believe in fate.

The world seems brighter now.
As if before I was painting in watercolours,
something has changed and now
I've struck the canvas with acrylics.

Monochrome met vibrancy
when I stumbled into you.

Caution: I'm broken
and sometimes my sharp edges
hurt the ones that get close.

Arms crossed,
it's not a barrier,
not a warning,
//Do Not Enter//

It's a knot
tied tightly
with careful hands
so I might not
u n r a v e l.

I know you believe I am an angel,
but my heart is not so kind.

If I am in any way,
I am an angel who's fallen.

Every time you tell me I am beautiful,
I long to show you all of the ways
in which my mind is not.

If you feel brave enough
to open my chest
with the sharpest of knives
in the hope that you could fix me,
please be gentle when
you meddle around with my heart.

I tell you you're smothering me,
choking out my flames.

You say I'm distant
and that I don't love you enough.

And we both break
because we both want this to work,
but these words, they hurt.

We need this though, this purge,
because this is how we grow.
This is how we'll get stronger.
This is how we'll get through this.

I really do love you.
I'm sorry that I'm an island.

Even you can't save me,
but I love all of the ways
in which you still try.

He broke me,
and I'm still surviving the heartache.

It'll be a war you'll have to fight
to break down these walls.
I've worked tirelessly
to build them so strong.
You see, the ones before
have bruised, battered, broken,
this worn out heart of mine.

I think it might heal
with some gracious time,
but until then there are bricks
stacked into the cloud cover
that you'll just have to climb over,
because I'm not quite ready
to let anyone through.

Sadness shoots a bullet
straight at your heart
and love buys you time.

There is no darkness,
there are no monsters,
the nightmares are gone,
when I have you.

"I can tell you're thinking about him again.
You always make a face."

"Oh, is it happy or sad?"

"Well, happy, because you're thinking about him.
Sad because you miss him."

Somehow,
despite our efforts,
we fall,
we live,
we love.

You are the light that overthrew my darkness,
the knight that stormed the castle gates
and slayed both the dragon that kept me captive,
and the demons that haunted me during my stay.

You still fought for me even when I boasted
that I could damn well save myself.

You give me hope on sleepless nights.

He made bedtime snacks for my monsters.

You thought I was beautiful
even though I wasn't dying,
while there was no tragedy
to make me lovely,
while the world wasn't worried
it would miss me.

Kiss me tenderly,
but if you take my breath away,
promise you'll help me catch it.

I've found a love that tucks me in tighter,
kisses my forehead for long heartbeat seconds,
a love that battles with nightmares
so I might find respite
on nights that are dark, gelid winters.

"Ever wish we could be innocent again?"
I asked you quietly.

"No," you started,
and then you kissed my neck
and nipped across my shoulders,
"because then we wouldn't be where we are now.
I think, for all of your scars, you're beautiful."

The stakes are high,
but your love is worth the risk.

Our candlelight was dimming,
the hours growing darker.
"Tell me you'll stay."

"I never planned on leaving."

My hands were cold
so you breathed
dragon puffs of smoke
in the winter
to warm them.

My heart was lonely
so you loved it.

What do we do now that I'm whole?
Is this what they call ever after?

I did not understand
the depth of falling in love
until I drowned in yours.

The sun is a blazing inferno.
The stars still shine in the day.
And I am in love with you.

- *Things I know to be true.*

There are so many
millions of ways
in which I am in awe of you,
but the only words
I can seem to find
to tell you this
are simply,
"I love you."

It's the little things,
sometimes it's the big things,
but in the grand scheme of things,
the things you do,
all of the ways in which
you put your heart out there,
all of the ways that you try
and try again,
a g a i n,
and again, and again,
those little things,
sometimes the big things,
the gestures,
the glances stolen,
the ways in which
you say you love me,
all of these things
steal my breath away,
so don't mind me if I'm left here
simply
gasping.

HOME

All of the words
I've not yet written,
they all belong to you.

Perhaps we don't have
all of the time in the world.

I believe though,
that what we're given
will be exactly enough.

If I could,
I'd hold on forever.

Because I can't,
I'll just hold on for now.

"I really have to get going,"
you whispered between breathless kisses.

Always one more before we parted.

Before the sun set too quickly
and the day was done, you called.

I heard the smile in your voice,
"Had I stayed, I would have kissed you
until the sun came up."

If this darkness
smudges the sunrise,
covers the distant mountains in grey,
stay with me.

Until the storm clouds break,
stay until the last of the thunder
rumbles away.

I want to feel the dewy grass
beneath my bare and muddy feet.
Let me slip as I spin
and take my breath away
when you catch me.

I want to carve our love story into trees,
beg them to tell the next souls
who wander here that love exists,
and ours, ours was fearless.

I have never loved so boldly before,
but you bring out the best in me.
The stars are jealous of all we've become.
We are alive with hair fraying
from the electric current running between us.
There are tears in our shirts
from branches trying to hold us here.
They know that we could live like this forever.

Kiss me until my lips are chapped
and stinging when I smile.
A love like this, an ethereal,
once in a lifetime love like this,
it's heady,
and I'll never be ready to come down.

Time spent with you,
well it's left me entirely mad.

There's not a day
that passes now in which
I am not crazily in love
with all that you are
and all you have yet to become.

We had coffee at midnight
so we could stay awake until sunrise
because no amount of time together ever satisfies.

Love is warm.
It's a fire burning bright
against snowflakes tumbling,
ice throwing itself at you.

It's being tucked in
before you fall asleep.

It's a mantra.
You are safe,
you are mine.
I'll hold on to this,
to you,
forever.

It would be rather beautiful
to wake before the rest of the world,
watch the sunrise,
sip coffee sweetened with raw sugar
and think of you as I do.

- *While the world is sleeping*

If I had the world's time,
I'd still come home to you.

No matter how severe your storm,
I promise I'll stay.
I'll stay through howling winds
that whip my cheeks raw and red.

I'll stay through the scorching wildfires
that burn up my edges,
steal away bits of me that float up
into the black smoke sky
as bright embers fading far too quickly.

I will stay and I will hold you close
when the nights leave you shivering,
give you space when your heat
pushes you into a fiery rage.
I will stay and I will love you
in whichever way you crave.

I breathe to live in awe of you.

I want to pull you to my chest,
feel your heart beating with mine,
kiss your lips until they're bruised,
a gentle reminder that I'd been there.

I want to see the stars from where you are
and the moon too.
I want to look at their beauty
and know it is nothing against yours.

And your mind,
more than anything,
I want to know what keeps it awake,
what haunts your dreams
and leaves you restless.

I want to be the thing that eases the tension,
the space for you to breathe in.

Wherever you go,
please know
you have my heart with you.

Over tea with my sister,
I asked if I was any different
when I was with you than I was without.

"You're not terribly different," she said,
stirred in cream and sugar,
"but you're happier with him."

You are snowflakes on my tongue,
winter's icy breath on my cheek.

I would live within the confines
of the smallest snow globe,
let the world shake us,
and still settle down to sleep
in silhouettes of snow angels with you.

TO WALK ON MOONBEAMS

Again and
Again and
Again and
Again

This tired heart
Beats and
Beats and
Beats

Just for you
It goes on
It goes on

There's a special kind of way
that love fills up your lungs,
takes up too much space
and steals away the oxygen.

But for you I'd stand
on the edge of mortality,
because what's the point of breathing
if it's not in hungry gasps?

Your love,
that brilliant kind of love,
it leaves me insatiable.

"Have you ever loved another
as you love me now?"

"I thought I had, in a time before,
but now that I know this love for you,
I fear I'd been terribly mistaken."

- *Blind is love*

BREATHE
I can't swallow this oxygen unless you do.

Time is not on our side,
but I will fight against it with you.

Our love consumes like wildfire.
We can't breathe through the heavy smoke,
but I'd choke on the pain to tell you
I never regretted loving you,
not for a second.

There's nothing else
I'd rather breathe for
than you, my darling.

I love the way you make me gasp and shiver.
I love the way you let me close my eyes
and rest in your gentle embrace.
I am in awe of the way
you let your walls down and love me.

There is nothing in this world,
nothing worth loving
as much as you are worth it.
For you I'll stay.
For you I'll carry on in this way,
keep breathing even if my breaths
become shallow and shaky at times.

It's all for you.
In every lifetime, it's always going to be you.

If this is our last sunrise,
I'll ignore the brilliant colours,
the reds, and pinks, and yellows.

I'll ignore the crimson glare,
the pastel parting clouds,
the rays of light peeking into existence.

If this is our last sunrise,
my eyes only have time for you.

Dance with me through pastel sunsets,
until the early morning sun warms us,
until we've spun, and dipped, and chapped our lips
with kisses that make the stars jealous.

"I love weekends with you," I said,
curled up under your sheets
with nothing but the radio playing
on a lazy Sunday afternoon.

"I love every moment with you."
You nuzzled my neck,
left a trail of kisses across my fiery skin.

"Even Tuesdays?" I teased.

You looked up at me intently,
smirked and assured me,
"Even Wednesday mornings at 7 AM."

There is an undeniable beauty
in the darkness before the dawn,
an unmatched silence
preceding the birds' songs.
I wish to live forever
in moments like this with you.

All of these colours
and I'd still rather look at you.

The leaves are changing
and the world still knows
no beauty as great as yours.

When we grow old
and our bodies rust
like tired machines,
I will still love you then.

I have loved
many versions of you
and I've no doubt
I'll love the one that follows.

They say this is perfection,
looking into the eyes of the one you love,
stargazing,
falling asleep next to them,
breakfast in bed.
You spend the afternoon indoors,
close the curtains so the streamers of light
don't peek through.
It's like a movie theatre this way,
sip soda from the same straw,
make popcorn at home.
The buttons beep
as you press them on the microwave,
it burns but only at the edges.
The scent of salt and butter are enough,
cover up your mistakes,
and sweep them under the rug.
For now things are fine,
we will worry about it tomorrow,
we will change the settings later.
The sun sets and together you prowl,
wander the city and sightsee.
The sky is painted like cotton candy fluff
and like this the world has never tasted sweeter.
Love like this, they say,
it's simple,
it's easy,
it's perfect.
Hold on they say.
Hold on.

End

About The Author

Shelby Marie is a poet and small business owner
from Ontario, Canada. When she's not writing poetry,
you'll often find her cozy with a book and snuggled up
with her darling tuxedo cat, Jaximus.

Keep in Touch

Instagram: @shelbymarie.poetry
TikTok: @shelbymariepoetry
Facebook Page: Shelby Marie Poetry

Visit the Shop

Check out Shelby's online shop
for more original poetry and handcrafted gifts.
www.shelbymariepoetry.ca

Leave a Review

If you enjoyed reading
To Walk on Moonbeams,
please consider leaving a review
on Amazon and Goodreads.

Thank you for taking such great care
of the paper pieces of my heart.

Much love, Shelby

SHELBY MARIE

Printed in Great Britain
by Amazon